T0192905

The Census Taker

The Census Taker

STORIES OF A TRAVELER
IN INDIA AND NEPAL

Marilyn Stablein

Black Heron Press
SEATTLE

Published by
Black Heron Press
P.O. Box 95676
Seattle, Washington 98145

10   9   8   7   6   5   4   3

The Census Taker
was originally published by
Madrona Publishers, Inc.
Book & Cover Design by
William James

Library of Congress Cataloging in Publication Data
Stablein, Marilyn
The census taker.
1. Title
PS3569.T127C4   1985   813'.54   85-10641
ISBN 0-930773-23-3

Acknowledgments

Grateful acknowledgment is made to the editors of the following publications where some of the stories or portions of the stories were first published: *Mississippi Review, Crazyhorse, Periodics, Willow Springs Magazine, The Fault, The Stone, Clinton Street Quarterly, Domestic Crude, Skyviews, The Arts,* and *Open Sky.*

The Dhobi stories appeared as a Wash 'n Press chapbook titled *Ticketless Traveler* in 1982.

"Mataji" received the Brazos fiction prize at the University of Houston, 1984.

I would like to thank the University of Houston for a Cullen Fellowship during which some of these stories were written.

The Census Taker was selected by Leslie Silko to win the King County (Washington) Arts Commission Publication Award in 1984. This publication is made possible by a grant from the KCAC.

ONE

I AM A Census Taker assigned to Bhotan – a country south of China, north of India and east of Tibet. It is a foreign assignment; I am the first woman posted here. The terrain is desolate and the dwellings remote. No previous Census records exist for Bhotan, so I've been instructed by my employers, the International Census Committee, to take a preliminary Census Survey. The information I gather will cover densities, practices and beliefs.

Useful Phrases

The phrases are incomplete but aid me in developing my own questions – questions I will submit to the committee after I complete the survey. The phrases are divided into three sections: Survival, The Interview, and Special Circumstances. I practice them with my servant. Sometimes he understands.

I. SURVIVAL, OR BASIC CONVERSATIONS
  WITH SERVANT
  You will come with me.
  I will pay you.
  Bring the map.
  Are your hands clean?
  Go fetch the china.
  Fill the teapot at the lake.
  Put the pot on the fire.
  Take it off.
  Unless I tell you, do not bring wood.
  When the sun sets, light the fire.
  Do you have flint?

  Pitch my tent here.
  Saddle the yak.
  Lay the cloth.
  Will that caravan return?
  Unless all the work is done, don't go.
  You must not go.
  I forbid you to go.
  Come back!
  Clean this!
  Wash it with sand.
  Filter the milk through the filtering cloth.
  The kettle leaks. Is there a blacksmith?

II. The Interview

Please finish your soup.

Do not get up.

I am thirsty.

How many are you? Or, what are your numbers?

Do you smoke?

Chew?

Snuff?

What medicine is this?

How many marriages? How many brides?

Why are you childless?

Do you have sex?

How do you have it?

Can you show me?

What does that mean?

Do your children smoke?

How old are you? Is he? Is she?

Do you worship?

How do you worship? And what?

Can you spell that please?

Once more, and slower.

One final time, if you will.

Here is your receipt.

You are very kind.

Write to me. I will send you my photograph.

III. SPECIAL CIRCUMSTANCES
Thank you, but I am already married.
One husband is enough for me.
My husband is jealous.
You are not to come.
You are unwelcome.
Please retire.
You must desist.
I am asking that you desist.
My servant will show you out.
Do not be rude.
I have nothing of value.
You may not have this.
I am warning you to stop.
You will be sorry.
I am armed and a good shot.

On Husbands

To determine the number of people living in a household, I must pose the Census questions in such a way as not to mention husbands. This is easy, I learn, since there is no word for husband in the language of Bhotan. Brush and comb, saddle and blanket, knife and sheath are some of the metaphors for husband and wife. It took me some time to learn this. Women would ask me, "Where is your brush? Where is your saddle? Where is your hunting knife?" and then burst out in peals of giggles before I could answer correctly, "Back home. I left it, him, actually, back home."

Marriage is customary in Bhotan. The women dress in silk brocades, don gold nose rings, and shuffle in embroidered slippers to the temples. They go in large, giggling groups. The men throw paper charms and wish them luck.

Women don't marry men in Bhotan. They marry surrogates. That way they will never be lonely and will always have one husband intact. The surrogates are *bel* fruits. In addition to a *bel* fruit, a woman may marry a man and all of his brothers, too. It is the custom. But the only official marriage, the only one that is legal, is the *bel* fruit marriage. That way if the other husbands die or desert, a woman will always have her surrogate husband. Spinsters and widows do not exist.

I have been advised to marry. I consider it. I am fond of weddings but the words, "One husband is enough," keep coming to mind. When I speak these words, however, no one is convinced. Then I learn that the word I am using for husband is actually "*bel* fruit," so when I say, "One *bel* fruit is enough..." everyone agrees. One *is* enough. But where is mine?

At the market I shop for a *bel* fruit. The *bel* fruit that women marry are dehydrated and very brittle. I pick one up. It is only a quarter of the size of the fleshy kind. Its surface is firm, round, like sandpaper. I sniff, rub, and fondle. It is light and an ugly dull color.

The merchant tosses a dried *bel* fruit into the air and catches it. "Because they are dessicated," he says, "they will never spoil. The larger ones, however, crack easily," he warns. Boxes come with the *bel* fruits: sandalwood, ebony, or teak lined with uncarded lamb's wool. The boxes are soft and protective on the inside but have dirty feathers pasted on the outside to outwit thieves.

Plunge

In the *Foreign Language Daily* I buy in the bazaar, I skim the pages for news: conquests, insurrections, plagues. What intrigues me most is the plunging bus. Today it is "50 Die in Plunge." Yesterday it was "Bus Plunges Off Bridge," before that "Pilgrim Bus Plunges Enroute to Festival." The paper is not current. It arrives on camel caravans from the south. It arrives regularly, but months late. Curiously, it is always a southern country where these buses take their plunges; there are always many deaths.

I can think of a number of explanations. It could be that this newspaper only receives the news from one country and that there are probably just as many plunging buses in other places. Or, maybe in this country there are no trains or planes, and consequently there are twice as many buses so that the number of plunging ones is actually quite small in comparison to the regular, or non-plunging, ones. It could also be that the peasants of this southern country never learned to swim so that when a bus leaves the road for the waters of some lake, it is not the bus injuries that cause death, death comes from drowning.

There are other choices besides plunge: careen, skid too close to the edge, or even is forced off the road. To say that a bus crashes is too blunt. No one would read about crashes with any interest. Crashes are common and don't imply elevation. Furthermore, crash is the end result, the infamous end of the plunge. To say, on the other hand, that "Pilgrims Atop Bus Die in Plunge" adds a metaphysical sense, as if they somehow died mid-air.

It seems the reporter, like me, has developed an affinity for the plunge. A plunge is definitely more romantic than a fall. In a fall there is a clumsiness or haphazardness. Plunge, on the other hand, suggests intention. Destiny or fate is absent. It could almost be as if there were a desire to plunge inherent in the bus itself, a sort of free-fall urge. As with whales who mysteriously beach themselves on a shore, out of their element, maybe there is a fleet of buses that instinctively seeks the shortest route down, the glorious plunge – buses which risk all for that brief airborne ecstasy.

Measures

I visit a tailor. He sits cross-legged on a cushion turning a hand-powered sewing machine. He gives it a good push, lets it spin a few times, then turns it again. He stops spinning and looks up when I come into the shop. The machine slowly comes to a halt.

"I need winter clothing," I begin. "Something warm for a journey north."

He is silent for some time, then he answers. "A *chuba*. You would be warm in a *chuba*." He nods out of the open door to a group of women. They wear long, woolen jumpers belted at the waist. "*Chuba*," he confirms. It is the native dress – the women's arms, legs, and necks are covered, as well as the rest of their bodies. Only their faces and hands are bare.

"I'll measure you, but you must undress."

"Can't you measure over this?" I gesture toward my clothes.

He shakes his head. "It will not work."

I undress. He nears me with an abacus in his hand.

"How can you measure with that?" I ask.

"This only keeps a record," the tailor replies. "I measure with my hands."

"With your hands?"

He nods.

"Don't you have a measuring tape?"

"No. We don't use measuring tape. In Bhotan we use the body to measure. Do you see those pilgrims outstretched on the road?" He glances out the door. "They travel that way, marking the ground with their bodies. It is a form of respect and a form of measuring. Distances are measured by the number of prostrations from temple to temple. Now, please let's begin."

He places his finger first on one arm, then the other. He measures the length of my feet, the bridge of my nose, the circumference of my elbows, by placing his fingers, one next to another. Sometimes he measures twice if there is a finger's discrepancy. There is no place he does not touch with his meticulous fingering. I get goosebumps.

"Never mind," he says. "I am almost finished."

The neck is the basic unit: arm length, leg length are measured in units of necks. My neck is twenty-eight fingers around — he counts it on the abacus. My height is ten times this. He mumbles.

"What is that?" I ask.

"So tall," he says. "You are so tall."

He wouldn't say that, I think, if he weren't so short.

I return in three days and try on the *chuba*. It is the same tentlike jumper that all the women wear. Even the size is standard, only the tailor has added an eighteen-inch band of cloth to the bottom to compensate for my height. I don't like the ugly seam or the patchwork effect.

"All that measuring," I complain. "This band is only tacked on. Couldn't you make it more fitting?"

"Fitting?" he asks. "Of course, fitting. Let me measure again for fitting."

Conversation with a Lama

From the monastery roof I can see the rice-ter-raced mountain spreading out below me like a woman's gathered skirt. The lama's servant calls me. I follow him. At the door to the lama's room I pause briefly, then part the thick drape. He motions to a carpet and I sit down. The servant brings me a pillow.

"So, you are the foreigner – the one with an abacus," the lama asks.

"No. I don't have an abacus, but counting is my job. I'm a Census Taker on assignment here."

"And you don't use an abacus?"

"No."

"What do you use?"

"I don't use anything. I just take notes. When I finish collecting data, then I'll add up the numbers."

"You could use a rosary."

"What for?"

"For counting."

"It won't work. The numbers I collect will be greater than the number of beads on a rosary."

"Greater than hundreds of thousands?"

"I don't know. I haven't finished counting yet."

"With a rosary like mine you can count hundreds of thousands. You just pull down a brass bead on this leather thong attached to the rosary. See, there are two thongs: one measures hundreds, the other thousands."

"I like your system...but I'm not counting prayers. I count people. It might work, but I doubt it."

"People don't need counting."

"They do. It's important to keep records: births, deaths..."

"How do you count people?"

"It's easy. One person, one count."

"But people never stay put. Nor do they congregate in one place. They move back and forth. How do you count them? All of them?"

"I'll travel to them. I have a servant with me. We have four yaks loaded with supplies. We'll travel for six months throughout the country. At each house I'll record Census data. I'll even count nomads."

"Where will you find them?"

"I'll ask along the trail. My servant's brother is a caravan guide. He knows every trail."

"I see... that means you count mothers, sisters, husbands, and children, too?"

"I'll count everyone."

"But what if a woman, for example, is a mother to a child, a wife to a husband and a sister to a brother? How many is that?"

"Just one. One body, one count."

"I'm glad you said that. Bodies *are* important. I make that distinction, too. Non-bodies are also important — but not as much."

"Non-bodies? What do you mean by non-bodies? Nobodies! You mean nobodies?"

"Non-bodies are beings without bodies. Maybe they'll get bodies in their next birth; or, maybe they had bodies in their last incarnation. But for this lifespan, they are without bodies. Being they have.... Take rocks, for instance. They have being and even feelings. Some have spirits, voices, and pulse."

"Rocks with being? I've seen some colorful rocks but I've never seen one with pulse."

"It's unfortunate."

"What's unfortunate?"

"Rock births. To be reborn a rock without a body — it's one of the least desirable rebirths you can have. It depends on karma, of course. Where did you say you are from?"

"America."

"Is that south of the Lung Po?"

"That's a river, isn't it? No. America is another country. Over to the west and across an ocean. You must have heard of it."

"I've heard of it: *A Me Ri Ka, A Me Ri Ka* ...*AAhhh* is an expiration of breath with a sound to it; *Me* is fire; *Ri* is mountain and *Ka* is mouth. Ah, Fire Mountain Mouth — it sounds like a volcano."

"Do you have a map?"

"No."

"I'll sketch one here on the floor for you. We're here. If you travel overland for, say, three months, cross the Ganges, over the Khyber, the Bosphorus, the Atlantic Ocean..."

"I know oceans: ocean of regret, ocean of rebirth, of tears..."

"This one is water. Like salty tears, but larger than any lake. Waves like thunder —"

"So, what do you want?"

"What do I want? There are many things I'd like

to ask you. But I'll limit myself to Census questions."

"Why?"

"That's my job — asking questions and counting."

"Ask me some questions. What kind of questions do you ask?"

"How many monks live here? How old are you? How old is the monastery? How far is the next village? Do you grow food? Are you in good health? Are there any nuns?"

"I like your questions. They are very nice."

"Can you answer?"

"What?"

"The questions. Of course, I'd like you to answer them."

"Do you have any more?"

"I always have more questions. How can I learn if I don't ask questions?"

"You're right. I like you. I like your questions. Don't be afraid to ask questions of me."

"Thank you. So, how many monks live in your monastery?"

"You want me to answer?"

"Of course, that's why I ask."

"You didn't tell me you wanted answers."

"What did you think I wanted?"

"To ask questions."

"You mean you thought I only wanted to ask and not get answers?"

"I only thought what you said — that you wanted to ask questions. About the number of monks: there are monks with being and monks with non-being; there are beings that are non-monks and likewise for nuns. Do you see the problem?"

"Just a simple head count. You can give me a rough idea. To put it bluntly, how many bodies reside here? Forget about being for now. How many living, breathing, human bodies?"

"I can't answer that."

"Why?"

"You assume bodies are finite. I do not."

"I only assume you can count the monks. How many meals do you serve? How many rooms, how many cots are there? How many — "

"Keep going. I like your questions."

"How many shoes outside the temple door? How many offerings on the shrine? How many butter lamps are lit each night?"

"Yes, go on. Ask more questions…"

"Why do you sit all alone? Why do you count prayers? Where did my servant go? Why do you smile at my questions? Why don't you answer me? Why are there rocks on your altar?"

Road Gangs

Many countries border Bhotan. Some are friendly, some are suspect. One is building a road across the interior. There are no motor vehicles in Bhotan but when the road is finished, trucks bearing refrigerators have been promised. Why refrigerators when ice is easily available? No one will say.

We approach a road gang at work. The road workers are women. Ribboned braids crown their heads and coarse wool the color of dust tents their bodies. They wear high-topped gym shoes two sizes too large and four layers of socks. One tells me she makes more working on the roads than she did pounding tea into bricks, but the hours are twice as long.

The women line up in pairs: one of the pair holds a shovel, the other woman holds a rope fastened to the wooden handle. My servant and I watch. After the first woman drives her shovel into the ground, the other pulls on the rope. It is easier to shove and pull than it is to lift and carry. With the work shared like this, it takes twice as many workers working half as hard.

My servant tells me the ground is leveled each autumn but mud slides cover the roadway during the following monsoon. Trees and grasses once kept the higher ground intact, but they have been cut to fuel the stoves of the road gangs and feed the livestock of the builders. Every year the road gangs uncover the mud slides and chop more trees. Every year the mud slides grow larger.

TWO

I FIRST met Mataji at the river. I had traveled a long way by bus, boat, and truck. The Middle Eastern countries were hard to travel through. I was pelted with rocks once. Women just don't travel alone in Muslim areas. The river at Benares seemed hospitable in comparison, a natural stopping point. A time to recoup, write home. Hindus came to Benares to die. Me, I just wanted to settle myself.

Jeans are unsuitable in hot climates. My sweat moistened the cloth and the usual pert denim stiffness became saggy and limp. The cloth soon chafed the skin on my legs raw. When I couldn't stand the soreness any longer, I left the pants on the bank of the river and waded in up to my waist. A crowd of men with nothing better to do gathered; I didn't want to come out of the water and expose my bare legs. That's when Mataji appeared. She stood on the bank and raised her voice in an incomprehensible tirade; the men reluctantly backed off. I was grateful. She led me to her campsite and handed me a piece of orange cloth that was folded in her knapsack. I dumbly held the material.

"Put it on," she said.

I tried to tie it around my waist like a bath towel, but Mataji scowled. She made me take off my T-shirt and tied the cloth on me herself, wrapping the pleated part with a long swoop. Her manner didn't embarrass me. Even when her brown hand cupped one of my breasts from underneath and she asked if I had any children. She jiggled the flesh to ascertain if the breast had held milk or not.

"Children?" she repeated.

"No. No children."

Mataji helped me find a room after I tried camping out with her for three days. The room was in back of a Shiva temple, and I could reach the burning *ghat* where Mataji camped in thirty minutes if I walked along the bank. During the rainy season I'd have to go through the bazaar, she warned me, and find the right alleyway leading down to the cremation ground, the most famous *ghat* in Benares.

Everything Mataji did was public: she bathed in the river, dusted her brown skin in cremation ash, cooked at a fire pit, and at night curled up in the sand on top of a cotton blanket and went to sleep. She didn't have a tent. If rain started to fall, she shifted to drier ground. Most of my days were spent with her but at night I needed to close a door behind me and lock it, so that I could go to sleep as I had always done, growing up in my mother's house.

I learned quickly. Soon I could bathe in the river in one piece of cloth and afterwards tie a fresh one over the dripping one; I could then wiggle out of one while hiding under the other. It was a discreet operation, though cumbersome. I'd say that about wearing a sari in general — discreet but cumbersome. I couldn't climb stairs, for instance, unless I held up the skirt of the sari. If my hands were full of bundles, the yardage held me back unless I could maneuver my hips to swing the cloth to one side and carefully place a foot down. If I stepped on the skirt, the material came loose from my waist, where it had been tucked. On a sari there are no zippers, buttons, snaps or hooks, just six unwieldy yards of cloth. In a sari I couldn't run or swim, but then the heat was too great to run in, and if I wanted to swim badly enough I could always enter the water fully bundled like the local women, ease out of the sari underwater and leave it bunched up on the steps as I swam naked. The water was murky, clogged with ash, and no one could see beneath the surface.

I had never been so preoccupied with keeping myself covered. But if I did cover up, stray men wouldn't bother me. Mother would laugh to see me here, covered from neck to ankle in cloth. I could hear her say, "What are you up to now?" or "Who do you think you are, Queen of Sheba?" I'd been meaning to write home but hadn't done it yet. I wondered if she'd believe me anyway. She'd have to believe the postmark: India. Wouldn't that scare her.

Mataji belonged to a Tantric sect of Shiva worshippers called *aghoras*. In a book on Hinduism I had read, the chapter on Tantra was the most interesting and the most sexy. One graphic temple carving depicted a woman standing on her left leg; the other leg gripped a man tightly to her hips, locking him there. I liked the assertiveness she showed, the force of her grip. Lying under a man, prone and crushed under his weight, well, I'd tried that.

Mataji was the opposite of sexy. I watched her in the bazaar drinking rotgut palm wine. She could outdrink and outshout the captain of police. Her teeth were corroded from chewing betel nuts, her spit bright crimson from the betel juice. She never combed her hair, now matted together in strands an inch thick and a yard long. Her camp-site above the cremation pyres was grotesque. Her mannerisms were tough. But a part of her religion, she explained, was to cultivate the grotesque so she could overcome fear of it.

We were the only women at the *ghat*; the other *sadhus* wore only loincloths. They all had waist-length matted hair. I would have been afraid by myself but with Mataji I could join in, smoke *ganja* and not feel too self-conscious about being the only young woman, and a foreigner, in a group of stoned, barely clothed ascetics.

"*Aghoras* eat anything, even shit," Mataji told me. "They sleep anywhere, meditate anywhere. For us there is no good, no bad, no fear, and no desire."

"What do you mean, eat shit?"

Mataji laughed, revealing her brown stained teeth. "You don't *have* to eat shit, but you shouldn't be afraid to. You'd be a good *aghora*, Prem," she said to me. "But I won't make you eat shit."

Mataji never called me by my given name; nor did she call me memsahib — that was too formal. "*Prem...lata...*that is a good name," she announced one day. I didn't know what the words meant until I looked them up in a Sanskrit dictionary much later. *Prem* is love, not a sexual love but a love for fellow beings, compassion; *lata* is a

[27]

creeping vine, a metaphor for a graceful slimness with an element of tenacity.

We gathered around Mataji's *dhuni*, fire pit. There were two older *sadhus*, a younger initiate, Mataji and me. Mataji fished a clay pipe out of the ashes with her tongs. She always put the pipes into the burning coals after we smoked; the fire burned off sediment. I moistened a clump of dried *ganja* leaves in one palm and kneaded it as Mataji had shown me, until the leaves had the consistency of paste. She rubbed a small amount between her fingers to test it. "*Tik hai,*" she confirmed.

The pipe was cylindrical and tapered from a bowl to a narrow mouthpiece. After I filled the pipe, I passed it to the *sadhu* on my right. He took coconut fibers from a husk and twisted them into a tight ball which he tossed into the fire. When the ball was aglow, he picked it up with the tongs and placed the burning mass atop the pipe. The *sadhu* on his right drew first, while the other pressed down on the burning husk. He offered the smoke to Shiva in a loud burst of prayer.

"She needs a partner," one of the *sadhus* said, nodding to me. "Mataji, how about me? I'd be a good partner for her." He stood up, chest inflated, and strutted around the fire.

"No, me, Mataji," the other cut in. He reached

over and grabbed the other's balls. "I'm more qualified."

"Hell you are..." the other retorted; they wrestled in fun. I was afraid they were going to compare penises. I snuggled into Mataji's lap, hiding my eyes in the cloth. I heard a yell. When I looked one had pinned the other down, the head perilously close to the fire.

"Stop it," Mataji commanded. "Go on, get out. You've had your smoke."

They left pushing each other back and forth. The young initiate stayed and I remained curled, my head on Mataji's lap. She swept my hair away from my face and began to inspect my scalp, which she liked to dust with ash to keep the lice away. One of the *sadhus* must have put opium into the *ganja*. I was too tired to walk back to my room that night. It was already late and I fell asleep where I was. Sometime in the middle of the night someone tossed a blanket over me. I assumed Mataji was covering me. But then a hand slid over my back and found a path leading over my hips, and I knew only a man could touch me that way. I could have protested but I didn't.

In the morning I was awakened by a police officer. He wasn't in uniform but he was asking for my visa.

"Where is your passport, memsahib?"

"Passport?" I rubbed my eyes. I couldn't believe a man was standing over me demanding my passport. The sun was barely in the sky.

"I don't have it here," I told him. "It's in my room."

"You have a room, memsahib?" he asked. "Then why are you sleeping here? Do you know these beggars are untouchables?"

"I don't have my passport here," I repeated, not wanting to get into an argument. Mataji was still asleep.

"I need to check it."

"'Well, I could bring the passport to your office. Do you have an office?"

"Of course I have an office. I could come to your room instead."

"No, thank you. I'll bring it."

He took down my name and passport number and then left. I closed my eyes again. The mournful death chant of a grieving family wound in and out of my dreams: *rama nama satya hai . . . rama nama . . . .*

The alleyways were dark and shady near the river. The buildings were so close together that the alleys were hemmed in by continuous walls. The path was only about six feet wide, sometimes less. I stopped to admire a stall draped in glass beads.

"Wait a minute," the merchant said, raising his eyebrows. His voice changed to a whisper. "I've got special beads. Look here." He uncovered a string of clear crystal, more like a rosary than a necklace. "They spark," he said. Suddenly he threw his shawl over us. Sure enough, in the dark space under the shawl, the beads, when two were struck together, sparked like a cigarette lighter out of fuel — the flame never caught. I liked the coolness of the stone.

"How much?" I asked.

"For you, a special price."

"I know. I know. It's always a special price."

"For you, memsahib, only fifty rupees."

Mataji was mad when I showed her the beads later that afternoon and told her what I paid.

"You never buy a *mala*," she fumed. "Don't you know that? You must be given a *mala*. A teacher gives you a *mala*. You don't buy one."

I felt sheepish and fell silent. She stormed back to the shop and argued with the merchant. He refused to return my money. There was a tug-of-war between Mataji and the merchant. The string broke and crystal balls flew everywhere; most landed on the dung-and-mud alley. When a police-man arrived, he had to push his way through the crowd that had gathered. Beggars on their hands and knees picked up stray beads, while women, their heads supporting large baskets of produce, shouted to be allowed through. Traffic in the alley came to a total standstill. Mataji was arrested by the same policeman who had checked my visa.

"Where are you taking Mataji?" I protested. "You can't arrest her. She didn't do anything wrong."

"She is always doing something wrong. This woman is no good. Everyone complains about her drinking, the trouble she causes. Stay away from her, that is my advice to you."

"I don't need any advice. What about my money? I bought the beads. Where's my refund? I want a refund. You can keep your advice. I want my money."

"You'll get the money," he sneered, "even if it comes out of her pocket." He tightened his grip on Mataji's arm. She looked terribly frail with the orange cotton cloth of a Hindu ascetic tied behind her neck. It covered her torso to the knees. The soles of her feet were like callused pads; years of walking barefoot had flattened her arches. The thick mass of her matted hair twisted around the top of her head, standing eight inches above her skull. Still, she was shorter than the officer.

"*Tik hai*," she reassured me. "He can't keep me."

The officer was about to lead her off but he stopped and addressed me. "Oh, about your pass- port, memsahib…"

"You saw it," I snapped.

"The captain says it's unacceptable."

"What do you mean unacceptable?"

"You need a permit."

"For what?"

"Americans, memsahib, need permits."

"That's the first I heard of it." I looked at Mataji but she was staring off into space. I could have challenged him further, but I didn't. I wandered around the bazaar and then angled down to the burning *ghat*. I smoked a pipe and waited. Mataji returned in two hours, very drunk.

"That was quick," I said.

"Humph," she scowled and then spit into the fire. "The captain wants to know about the sahib."

"What sahib?"

"Your sahib."

"I don't have a sahib."

"I *know* you don't have a sahib. That's what I told them. 'No sahib. She is not married, you fools.' But they wouldn't believe me. 'How can she be alone? She *must* be married.' Men always want to know where your husband is so they can slander or outwit him...until you get old like me. Then it's too late." She laughed and hiccupped at the same time. "They think I poisoned mine." She laughed so hard her eyes watered.

Mataji dried her eyes with a corner of her cloth and put a copper bucket onto the coals. She dipped a finger into the water, flicked it on the coals, and when there was barely a sizzle she spit again into the fire pit.

"Too cold, Prem. Go get me some coals. Jail is enough work for one day. I'm an old woman."

"Where would I get coals?"

"At the pyre, where else? I don't live at the burning *ghat* for nothing, you know." She stood up to get a better view of the funeral pyres. "There's a good one down there, Prem. Hurry. I'll make tea."

I felt helpless. "I can't get coals there," I spoke up. "Those are the coals of the dead. You can't cook with those."

"Coals are coals. The dead are dead; they won't mind. Are you going?"

I shook my head. She stomped off then with her tongs in hand. She walked down the sandy bank to the largest burning pyre and helped herself to a burning log. The attendants protested but Mataji could outshout a bullhorn in a riot; she ignored the protests. She returned to the fire pit and dropped the log in the middle; a cloud of ash rose in its wake. She swatted at the tiny particles as if they were a swarm of mayflies.

"Mataji?" It was nearly dusk. The leering face of the police officer reflected the glow of the fire. He also was drunk and almost stumbled into the pit.

"What do you want?" Her eyes narrowed and her nostrils widened. I could see the flame in her eyes.

"Just a friendly visit," he winked at me.

"We're not friends," I said. "You're bothering us."

"So you're a *sadhu* now, memsahib. You drink and smoke and wear their dirty rags, too."

"Get out of here," Mataji snarled.

The alcohol on his breath smelled like dead rats. He lunged toward me. "What would your mother think?" he said. "Why aren't you married? Would no man have you?"

I forced him away with my foot against his chest.

"I'm the mother here," Mataji boomed. "Have you no respect for mothers? You miserable bastard; your mother died happy the day you were born. You cheap, lusting fool. No respect for mothers!" Her voice grew louder with each sentence, louder than a locomotive crossing a steel bridge. The muscles in her neck grew tight; her eyes were wild.

"No respect for mothers! The Devil curse you. Out! Out! Out of my camp, you bastard!"

The officer drew back for a moment, then pulled at my arm, loosening the sari on my shoulder. Mataji picked up my shoe and beat him with it. The same *sadhus* who had smoked our pipe came over, hearing the ruckus. The officer cowered under Mataji's knocks. To be hit by a shoe, especially by a lower-caste woman, was a deep insult. Mataji called upon the demons of her sect to tie and bind this offender.

"I've come to arrest the memsahib," he blurted out. He stood up and fumbled in his pocket for some papers. "She is in violation of—" He couldn't finish his sentence because a *sadhu* threw ash into his eyes. Another jabbed him with his Shiva trident and soon *sadhu* justice prevailed. The officer was booted out of the camp and stones followed him till he was out of sight. We lit a large pipe and everyone drew on it as it passed around the fire pit.

I left Benares about a week later. A French traveler told me I could get a new visa in Nepal and Mataji gave me the name of another *aghora sadhu* to look up. When I said goodby at the station she surprised me with a wooden *mala* and a glob of opium—the best defense against the third-class train ride. "Don't you know you never buy a *mala*," she said and laughed.

I thought about writing to her after I left but I had no address for her and she couldn't read anyway. Sometimes I thought about her — like the time I got lost in Orissa looking for a post office. I had been following a bullock cart trail but it abruptly broke off into three directions. Row after row of beach pine, planted as a hedge against hurricanes, looked exactly the same. Tired, thirsty, confused, I stumbled into a village in the middle of that forest and was soon surrounded by snarling dogs. It was a village of old women, grandmothers left home to watch the children while the parents toiled in the fields. They all had the same toothless grin, the boniness and the sagging breasts. One reached for my wrist.

"Bangles...where are your bangles?"

"Bangles," the others joined in, forming a tight circle around me. "Bangles...*kahan hai?*"

Every woman wore bangles, love tokens, gold for the rich, glass or plastic for the poor. No bangles whatsoever signaled no one loved a woman, no one possessed her...no brothers, no father, no husband. They started to talk among themselves.

"*Sati,*" one cried and the others echoed the chant: "*Sati, sati, sati.*"

"No," I protested. "I'm not a widow. I didn't tear off my bangles at my husband's pyre. I never had any bangles, nor have I had any husband. I'm a *sadhu*." I couldn't think of any other way to explain my bare arm, my situation. Then I remembered the *mala* in my bag and pulled it out. I pretended to recite some prayers. "I pray to your god," I said. "*Bhagavan* knows...I'm a *sadhu*." Oh, Mataji, I thought, you should be here now; show these women that a woman can live alone.

Shortly after that I heard from a *sadhu* I met at the train station that Mataji had died.

"Which Mataji?" I questioned him. "The one from Benares?"

"The one from Benares," he confirmed.

"Are you sure? Describe her," I demanded.

He said she was thin, her hair long and matted, her teeth stained and ugly.

"Yes. That sounds like her. Where did she live?"

"There's only one Mataji, the *aghora* Mataji," he said. "She always camped at the burning *ghat*."

I sat down on my knapsack and from that great distance I thought I could hear the same sad drone that I always heard at the burning *ghat*. The death chant: *rama nama satya hai...rama nama satya hai...rama nama satya hai....* But this time there was a larger crowd. *Sadhus* huddled together as if such closeness might lessen the loss, the grief. Instruments were played. The attendant kept busy poking the coals. Her corpse was laid atop the wooden pyre. There were never any caskets at the burning ground. Already the ash-sifters were arguing over who could sift through the remains for gold fillings or rings left on the body – but Mataji had no gold fillings or rings. Someone paid for the thin silk that wrapped her body briefly before it burned away and her body was exposed in its last hideous state. The attendant poked her leg back into the flame; the skin burst and juices oozed, sizzled and squirted. I knew that even her death was public. I shivered, not with disgust, but with an alertness.

THREE

IN India in the sixties I wore cotton saris and buffalo hide sandals called chappels. During the monsoon I wore molded-plastic shoes from Taiwan because the streets were always muddy; if a building had a faucet out front, I could stick my feet, shoes and all, under the tap and rinse before entering. In the mountains I wore Tibetan skirts and Chinese silk blouses cut and stitched to my size by my Muslim tailor. He was the first to call me "The Long-bodied Woman" – others began calling me by that name, but not to my face. I was so thin that my thighs were no wider than one-pound coffee tins.

I had a bit part in a Rita Tushingham movie called "The Guru." I played a hippie singing on a houseboat, only I sat at a window below the top deck and I didn't sing.

On my eighteenth birthday I fasted to curb desire and ego. I wanted to become enlightened; I was already a pacifist. I remembered the report on Gandhi I wrote in high school, the book *Siddhartha*, and the trilogy "Apu."

I had a Tibetan name meaning God Woman Life Happy.

I knew lamas in Sarnath, Bodh Gaya, Darjeeling, Dalhousie, Manali, and Kulu.

I spent hours reading, from the *Tibetan Dictionary*, such entries as "void" — there were eighteen definitions. There were the "void of eternal black," the "void of the windless expanse," the "void of regenerating emptiness," the "void of unrelenting confusion," and so on.

I taught myself the Tibetan script by copying the *Heart Sutra*. At each letter I drew in calligraphy I thought of the basic principle of the text: form is emptiness, emptiness is form. I copied the sutra onto folio pages I cut out of rice paper. I painted gold borders around the edges.

I memorized prayers to female saints and goddesses. I translated the twenty-one verses for Green Tara. I made a list of heroines I called "A Compendium of Females."

I went to the opening of the first disco in Delhi which coincided with the Moon Walk and danced until my sides ached.

I met a palmist who told me I had spent my

previous life in India. "You will have two children," he said. I kept in a notebook a vocabulary of divinations. I drew charts of the zodiac superimposed on a palm, a man's forehead, and a map of the orient.

I practiced geomancy, scattering pebbles on the ground to interpret meaning. A lama showed me how to throw the bones of a sheep and predict the weather; he also made predictions by looking at the way smoke rose from an incense stick, or the way a butter lamp flamed.

I was curious about but never saw haruspicy, divination by examining the entrails of animals.

I kept a dream log. I frequently dreamed about Tibet and the lamas I knew. I kept a separate diary of my dream life; I called the diary "Night Travels to Tibet."

I am a foreign diplomat assigned to Tibet. My airfare is paid by a government grant. The plane skims over glaciers and rock gorges. The pilot tells me: "O.K. Are you ready? Prepare to jump." There are no airports in Tibet. I jump. My gathered skirt billows and I hold a towel over me like an umbrella. It works. I descend with ease. Below me a tremendous waterfall appears but someone sees me coming and turns it off like a sprinkler. On landing my teeth rattle and I spit them out like chunks of glass. Lizards scramble for them. I follow a yak-herder into his tent. He feeds me. The soup has yarn and a weak pigeon in it. I question him on his taste. He asks me, "What is Tibet?"

I'm in the market for a quiet place. A real-estate agent shows me a cave. Inside I try on a bone apron for an audience of bats. The rattling echoes. I slice a cake shaped like Tibet — oblong and jagged with mounds of whipped cream. My knife sticks. I stand in line at a spigot outside to fill a bucket. In front of me is a long line of Tibetan women. The one I stand behind has long black braids; pink ribbons are tied and braided into her hair. She turns and hugs me. "Mother!" I exclaim.

I buy an old leather wallet from a beggar on the street. I like the texture; even the mold is authentic. Inside I uncover four fifty-cent coins. What luck! I get my money back. There is a folded paper in another flap. A Tibetan monk reads the words from a foreign script. It is a Tibetan shopping list: one pound of yak butter, three kilos of dried buffalo meat, two brick balls of tea, an astrological text...

There is no plastic in Tibet. I trade long rolls of plastic sandwich bags for frankincense and myrrh. I demonstrate a bag for every use: to store chilis, aspirin,

leaves, and stones. Suddenly everyone demands one.
I do not have enough to go around. Three lamas
explain they could keep rain water, powdered gold,
and spirit cookies in see-through bags. I wire home:
"Need more bags." A shipment is airlifted from
Delhi but comes apart in the air. Thousands of plastic
bags parachute to earth. The people catch them with
nets.

I ate ginger omelettes, chapatis, yoghurt, len-
tils, and drank boiled tea with milk every day for
three years. I picked wild saffron in the Himalayas.
It took me four days to collect enough stamens
from the fragile wild crocus to flavor one pot of
rice with saffron.

I washed pots at rivers using sand as a scouring
pad. Ash and straw worked just as well.

In Orissa on the coast village women taught me
how to forage for five kinds of wild plants, leaves
from hedges and trees, flowers, bulbs, and roots.
Food was scarce in Orissa. Rice was eaten three
times a day. I learned how to prepare rice in many
different ways: rice with cane sugar, milk rice,
boiled rice, fried rice, rice patties, rice cakes, rice
bread, rice custard, flattened rice with tea, puffed
rice with curry powder, popped rice, and rice noo-
dles. After one month I craved anything, anything
but rice. The fishermen brought me a sting ray

that got entangled in their nets. Did I want to eat it? The fish was too ugly for the villagers to eat; they called it a fish of the Devil. I hacked one into edible chunks with a dull knife. I hacked, ripped, and sawed for an hour. I simmered the fish for two hours in a pot on a cow-dung fire; the flesh was still chewy. I went back to eating rice.

I had a friend called Eight-Fingered Eddie who, sitting cross-legged in a houseboat, would go into a trance listening to scratchy Beatles tapes. He waved his arms and fingers in the air and called it dancing. He received checks in the mail from Uncle Sam and developed a following of ten.

I had a famous landlord named Tenzing who had a room full of Everest trophies, a room full of backpacking gear, gifts from the British government, and so many scrapbooks that he needed three trunks to hold them. Each trunk was wired with a heating device to keep the monsoon mold out. He had a disarming smile; his gaze alternated from a far-away stare to a roving eye.

I heard about but never met a junkie named Mayflower who had a pet monkey who was also a junkie. She had to hide her Bombay heroin in a locked metal box to keep the monkey from eating it all and overdosing. The monkey ate books, checks, money, and shoes.

I visited a yogi named Chen who hadn't left his

meditation cell in twenty years. I brought him homemade fudge as an offering, a patron's gift. He loved it. He wrote me three letters afterwards and he always mentioned the fudge: "with the blessings of the compassionate Buddha and your American fudge...." He published over a hundred pamphlets which he gave away free. One was called, "Welcome Hippies By this Way." He wrote a letter introducing me to his Chinese relatives in Calcutta. When I visited they served Chinese fish steamed in brown sauce and eight other dishes. The wife worked in a beauty parlor. One day she shampooed, set, and styled my hair. I looked different for three days.

I signed letters home "Seek Within" and "From the Vacuum of Liberating Chaos." Once, besides money, I requested a Japanese brush painting set, bikini underwear, preferably black, and a book on magic squares: "Send Immediately!" The package took four weeks to arrive and I had to pay the postman *baksheesh* to get it.

I met the man I would later marry in the bazaar in Benares when he asked me if I knew where he could buy a milk pail. I showed him.

I read the *Kama Sutra* and practiced making love cross-legged like the tantrics. I wondered why Indian men and women never hugged and why movies stars were not allowed to kiss on screen, although so many temples had explicit and highly erotic art. I compiled a list of positions for love-making and a chart of which positions the deities preferred, which worked for me and which were impossible or imaginary. I titled the information: "Concepts of (Sexual) Union." I made twenty-four entries — eight of which worked. On the outside of the notebook I wrote: གསང, the Tibetan for "Secret," because I didn't want anyone to read it.

On LSD once, I saw a cow calve. I perched on a balcony and kept my eyes on the alley below. The birthing took four hours and no one helped. The placenta glistened with more colors than a jellyfish.

I was the guest of a Maharajah who owned a highly prized strip of river-front property in one of the holiest cities in India. He knew how to smuggle meat into the strictly vegetarian town to impress his foreign guests. He introduced me to his guru — an Austrian with waist-length red hair who had lived in a cave in the Himalayas for fourteen years, spoke fluent Hindi, and preached Hinduism. He eyed me suspiciously.

I nicknamed a kid "Razor Blade Bob." He was so young and quiet that I couldn't believe his bandaged wounds were self-inflicted. He took *datura*, a plant that devotees offer to Shiva, and disappeared in the Ganges. The embassy investigated for a week but the kid with the bandaged wrists never reappeared.

Sitting next to an open window, I was once hit by a mud cake thrown at the moving train.

I hoarded white sugar and black-market kerosene because these were impossible to get when I needed them most.

I saw the Canadian ambassador take Buddhist vows under the Bodhi tree where Buddha was enlightened. Afterwards I went to meditate in a cave that was a day's walk away. I ate only seeds and dried fruit; in two days I was constipated and my legs stiff from sitting in that folded position. I stretched and watched a village-gathering in the valley below me. The people waved red flags and beat on drums. Voices rallied in unison. Then I realized it was a Communist demonstration.

I met many gurus. The Hare Krishna one asked me if I wanted to cut my hair and go to England to set up his center. I didn't. Another, who hadn't spoken in ten years because he had taken a vow to keep silent, scribbled messages on a chalk board. "Your *kundalini* is stirring," he wrote. "Now you must make it rise." One female saint sat on a dais while her devotees rubbed sandalwood oil on her feet and fed her milk-sweets. She wore thick, dark sunglasses at all times. One yogi proposed marriage and two refused to let me visit.

I received many initiations. Each initiation allowed me, or empowered me, to practice a different meditation. The Buddhist pantheon had hundreds of Buddhas and divinities to worship. I spent more time being initiated than I did practicing the meditations.

I knew the geographies of rivers, ponds, and streams. I knew the routes of trains, the maps of bazaars, and the itinerary of pilgrims. I traced from a book a map of ancient cave settlements; there were more than two hundred and nineteen sites, some with frescos, most without.

I read and copied from books on numerology, macrobiotics, and the sayings of Sufi prophets.

I drew mandalas, wore mandalas, and dreamed mandalas.

I never drove a car. I rode in three kinds of rickshaws: the motorized kind with a canvas top that looked like it belonged on a golf course, the bicycle rickshaw, and the rickshaw pulled by a muscular man in a loincloth and bare feet. I learned all the rates. I had an argument once with a city rickshaw wallah who wanted three times the usual rate. In anger I threw the money on the ground and pressed it into the dirt with my foot. Feet, in general, are strictly untouchable. He never picked up the money, nor did I.

A bullock cart ride I took once was so slow that I got out and walked.

I was frisked going into the Dalai Lama's reception room. I sat very still as Richard Alpert asked His Holiness if he thought the highest form of consciousness was like an acid trip. The Dalai Lama replied, "No." Outside we gave away mirror disks with stickum on the back and took Polaroid photographs that amazed the crowd.

I found a leech in a head of lettuce.

I saw the movie "2001" at a theater in Calcutta and cried. I sat through two showings. The air conditioning made me sneeze.

I taught English to a boy lama who, it was said, had "Om" etched on his teeth. This marked him as a reincarnated lama. I wondered if his permanent teeth would have "Om" on them, too.

I thought about becoming a Tibetan nun. I dressed like a pilgrim and when Tibetans asked me if I was a pilgrim I nodded yes. Once I covered the grounds of a temple prostrating like a pilgrim. Going up and down steps on my stomach was the hardest part. I also did 25,000 prostrations on a linoleum board I set up in my room. I wore waxed gloves to help my body slide up and down smoothly. At best, I did one hundred prostrations a day, keeping count with a rosary placed on the mat in front of me. Every time I lay on the ground, I shifted one bead on the string. My arms became very strong.

I dreamed Tibet was a province in California and I led a Peace Mission into the interior which was a ten-day walk from Lake Tahoe. At one monastery I was welcomed with a three-piece band – long horns and garish cymbals. I had a private room in the lamasery with my own shower, but it had no walls. Instead there were bleachers lining the shower room, which was underground. Every time I showered I worried: "Why am I naked in front of all these monks?"

FOUR

My summer retreat one year was a house in Kulu – that Himalayan valley paradise of glacier-fed rivers, mountain trout, wild honey, and hot springs. I rented a newly built house close to the river at the foot of a village. Behind me the houses rose like stepping stones up the hill.

A boy brought me water in two brass pots suspended by ropes from a yoke over his shoulders. That saved me from standing in line at the village spigot. I cherished my privacy, practiced oriental calligraphy, and learned bread-making using a single-burner kerosene stove. I found mica on a nearby path and collected it. Not knowing any embroidery stitches, I began to sew the flat mirror-like stones onto cotton with a cobweb effect: stitches zigzagged around each little disk, securing it in place.

Things changed after the first cow died that

summer. I then found out that my little cottage with the river view was actually bordering the burial grounds on the banks of the river. No wonder the village houses rose up the hill.

The first few days after a carcass was put out, only flies buzzed. But once the smell permeated the area, vultures would get wind of the putrid flesh. My river breeze carried the stench of death. A huge boulder in front of the house soon became the resting place of satiated scavengers. The birds literally ate so much they couldn't move except to perform some crazy wing-spread dance, shifting from one leg to another. Only after they digested the stuff and eliminated could they fly off – but that might take days.

So I welcomed the vultures, praised their function in the environment. The sooner they cleaned the bones, the better. I even incorporated the rotting flesh into my tantric meditations. After all, "life is impermanent," I'd remind myself each morning, lighting fresh incense sticks and checking the windows to see that they were tightly shut.

FIVE

In Kathmandu you can rent a room over a Tibetan restaurant called The Globe. The rent is $4.50 a month if you pay in U.S. currency or $8.00 in Nepalese currency. The room has a wooden floor, a woodframe rope cot and shutters on the windows instead of glass. The room is barely lit by an overhead bulb so you need to open the shutters for more light. Sometimes smoke from the restaurant kitchen comes in.

At night you can see the torchlight processions move up the cobblestone street. The Nepalese celebrate a festival throughout the valley every twelve years. All of the icons and statues that are usually hidden are then brought out, their clothes washed and pressed, their faces oiled with coconut oil and then dusted with rice flour. One day a year one hundred and fifty water buffalos are beheaded each with a single blow from a gurkha knife. The streets are littered with corpses. You may find your entryway, the door leading to the staircase to the second floor, blocked by a huge buffalo carcass. If you step on the body to get to the door, it will feel rubbery and firm at the same time.

You will eat water buffalo meat and drink boiled water buffalo milk: buff burgers at Aunt Jane's restaurant, buff mo-mos which are the Tibetan won-tons, and buff steaks at The Globe. The water buffalo cream is very thick. The cook argues with the milkman in the back alley every morning at 5:30. "Where's the cream? You thief! I will not pay for water. Water is free!"

A Tibetan astrologer eats regularly at The Globe. He has long matted hair and a loose cloth draped over one shoulder. "Cotton-clad" the cook calls him. The yogis wear cotton in the cold winter months to demonstrate their ability to keep warm with little or nothing on. "People born in the Fire Dog year," the astrologer says, "favor Mondays. On Mondays you should wash your hair, take a bath, trim your nails, sew yak curtains, and receive bloodlettings." He continues. "In addition, Tuesdays and Fridays are the best days to perform fire ceremonies, recite mantras, and begin a journey."

There are other shops on the street. At the yoghurt shop a man sits cross-legged wearing a t-shirt and *dhoti* and stirs a huge cauldron of foaming milk. He ladles the milk into thick earthen bowls. As the yoghurt sets, black soot settles on the skin-like surface and gives the yoghurt a smoky flavor. At the government hash store three grades of Himalayan hashish are molded into bricks, each stamped with His Majesty's Government of Nepal official seal.

You will learn to fold your hands together as if in prayer and say the word *namaste*. *Namaste* to the cook, *namaste* to the washerman, *namaste* to the Tibetan monk. On meeting and parting, *namaste, namaste*. The faces of the Nepalis light up like butter lamps when you salute them with *namaste*. "Di Di (sister) speaks Nepali!"

DON'T EAT ANY GREENS. BOIL WATER FOR TWENTY MINUTES the Peace Corps warns in large boldface letters on the bulletin board of the American Library. Diseases you can expect to be exposed to: chickenpox, malaria, giardia, smallpox, rabies, measles, hepatitis, jaundice, tubercu-lololosis. Common parasites: round worm, pin worm, hook worm, tape worm, liver flukes.

The city of Kathmandu lies at the bottom of an ancient lake bed. A deity, Manjushri, slit open the mountain to the south with his sword called Wisdom and drained the lake many æons ago. A river, the Bagmati, flows out of that crevice. The valley is a basin and every kind of garbage washes down into it. Night soil is used as fertilizer so even the sewage gets recycled back into the ground. It is said that amœbas and parasites outnumber the residents a billion to one. Nepalis try to charm away illness with black magic and witchcraft. The Tibetans do not believe in killing any living creature. "Germs have a right to live, too," they say.

Some numbers: *ek, doe, teen, char, paunch*... Nepalese for one, two, three, four, five. In Tibetan: *chik, knee, soom, she, nah*.

Knickknacks for sale in the bazaar: brass candleholders, hash pipes carved from soapstone, bronze Buddhas in any size or shape: two-armed, four-armed, sixteen-armed; yak amulets to protect the animals from catastrophe and to protect the owners from unruly yaks, charms to prevent scorpion bites, bone prayer beads, human thighbones made into trumpets and bowls carved from human skulls, incense twigs, woodblock prints on rice paper, gurkha knives that look like machetes, yak-hair woven blankets, and Tibetan saddle carpets.

The first phrases you memorize: This is too much. This is not fresh. I am not rich. I'll give you half of that price. It is rotten. Which way to: the bank? the post office? the embassy? the hospital?

Other Visitors and Tourists: a motorcyclist motors up the Everest Trail; royalty on safaris shoot endangered tigers in the *terai*; smugglers kill rhinos for the horns which are sold to the Chinese who claim the pulverized horn is an aphrodisiac.

There is a resort in the shadow of Mount Everest. Patrons fly in from Kathmandu and sip imported coffee for $3.00 a cup and watch muleteers and climbing expeditions pass by the picture windows, exhausted from the seven-day trek. A new enterprise has developed around the patrons — begging. It is so profitable that farmers are reluctant to tend their fields which get smaller each year anyway because of eroding terraces. Food in the high elevations is now in short supply.

Every dusk the Buddhists circle the holy mountain Swayambhunath. You can see the famous Monkey Temple on top from your window. The towering spire has eyes painted in the four directions. Elongated, the eyes are larger than dolphins. The monkeys on the mountain are aggressive. They snatch cameras, food, and rosaries out of the hands of tourists and pilgrims. The merchants at the bottom of the mountain keep slingshots in their back pockets, and when the monkeys sneak up and snatch a handful of corn, they have to be quick to outrun the stones from the slingshots.

When a monk comes into the restaurant, you cannot smoke. "God slayer" the cook warns. "He will call you a god slayer." The Tibetans believe that smoke from cigarettes kills those delicate sky creatures called *gandharvas* — the ones pictured in murals as plucking harps and carrying festoons of flowers at the time of great events like a Buddha's sermon. *Dakinis* and other helpful winged spirits are also smothered by the smoke from the tobacco plant. "What's worse," the cook says, "is legend says this poisonous weed grows where the menstrual blood of female demons falls to the ground."

Fact: the Buddha was born in Nepal. He left his footprints embedded in stone. They are over two feet long. A rubbing of the footprints hangs in the restaurant.

To bathe you can heat a bucket of water on the wood-burning kitchen stove and carry the bucket and a tin cup to the roof. You dip the cup into the bucket and pour small amounts of water over you. You can bathe with a single bucketful, or you can go to Balaju, a spring-fed bathing pool in the Queen's forest. There water pours out of a dragon's mouth and is contained in the pool. Sherpas stop off to bathe there on their way down from the high mountain trails. Or, you can bathe in the river if you keep your clothes on.

There are animal sacrifices at Dakshin Kali, a temple on the outskirts of the city. The villagers sacrifice animals they would normally eat. They bring their goats and chickens to the temple of Kali and slaughter them there, pouring fresh blood on the goddess's shrine. If you remember that the sacrifice is just a ritualized butchering like the water buffalo on the streets, it doesn't seem so bad. One spring the King ordered the sacrifice of five goats to ensure the safety of the Royal Nepal Airlines fleet of planes after a winter season when three planes crashed within a month.

Favorite fruits to buy from the merchant who squats on the street at the corner of the block: fresh lichee, mangos, and guavas. The lichee are sold by the branch. You won't recognize the fruit until you learn to rub off the papery sac surrounding the pearly flesh. *Nashpatti*s are good, too. They ripen in the fall. The fruit is crisp like an apple but juicier than a pear.

If there is a difference between yesterday and tomorrow it's hard to determine what it is. The Nepalis use the same word for both. The Tibetans have a saying, also, accompanied by a shrug, "tomorrow, day after tomorrow, what's the difference?"

In Tibetan the word for "work," *layka*, is used in a colloquial sense to mean "making love." So when someone says "I've got work to do," you will wonder which kind.

Even the wind has a tongue. Prayers are printed on flags and strung across monastery roofs and stretched from roof to roof on the tall buildings lining the streets in the old section of Kathmandu. The flags are called Horses of the Wind. When the movement of air flaps the banners, the prayers recite and bring good luck.

There is a temple three doors down from The Globe. The tiered roof looks like a utensil shop display. Brass trays, copper ladles, pots, lids, goblets, and cooking utensils have been attached to the roof by the patrons to celebrate domestic life. Marriage parades pass by your window. The groom rides a horse at the front of the procession now enroute to the bride's house after offering prayers at the temple. Behind the groom the dowry is displayed: chests of linens, chairs carried by servants, and even the marriage bed, a double-size rope cot borne on the heads of barefoot men.

There is a palace in the old part of Kathmandu where a young girl lives who is worshipped as a living goddess until she reaches puberty. Late at night her pale face can be seen peering out from one of the ornate wooden-sculpted windows. Her feet never touch the ground while she is in residence. Once a year the resident *Kumari* goddess is carried on a palanquin in a procession. Some *Kumaris* never learn how to walk until they are expelled from the palace once they menstruate. A *Kumari* is allowed to marry when she leaves the palace, but it is said that marriage to a dethroned goddess brings bad luck, so many become spinsters.

SIX

What is Compassion to a Fish?

Fɪsʜ in India, like cows, often lead privileged lives. It is even considered lucky to be reborn a fish in a sacred lake or pond where one is treated royally, fed with offerings for the gods, able to swim unmolested, to live to a ripe old age.

In Bodh Gaya there are fishmongers who cater to the pilgrim trade. For a modest sum a fish can be purchased from them and set free. The merit of such a compassionate act increases the pilgrim's chances for a better rebirth.

Dhobi watched pilgrims from many regions converge upon the village in great numbers doling out compassion, as alms for the poor. In shopping for merit, some unusual questions arise. Do fish have souls? Do larger fish have greater souls? What is compassion to a fish? Indeed, the good

[71]

intentions of the pilgrims are laudable.

But the fish? Each two-rupee liberation finds them cast loose in the same pond from which they were caught, as no rivers flow out of the village. So the fish make the rounds from the pond to the buckets and back to the pond again. There's no telling just how many times a fish has been liberated.

The Burning Ghat

Dhobi was accustomed to washing his customers' clothes on the *ghat* just upstream from the burning *ghat*. It is hard enough getting them clean and spotless with only a wooden paddle and a bar of Sunlight Soap, but when the water is flecked with ashes and other remnants of the dead, it is more difficult still.

Inexplicably, the current reversed itself on certain days and garlands of marigolds, rose petals, and lighted clay lamps balanced in boats of dried leaves pinned together with toothpicks floated upstream by Dhobi's *ghat*. He took this to be an omen and quickly immersed himself in the soothing waters of the Ganges. With a brass pot he poured water on his head like Shiva who received the sacred waters from heaven on his matted locks. The melodious names of Bhagavan blended with the ringing temple bells.

Once Dhobi was so entranced that he didn't notice a herd of water buffalo easing into the shimmering liquid beside him. He was just at the point of visualizing a confrontation with the Black Lord of Death, accounting for his unintentional sins and pleading for mercy, when a loud *moo-ooo* rang out. A startled Dhobi opened his eyes to a monstrous black face with bulging eyes and long whiskers. He fell to his knees, the water now up to his chin, and pleaded with the water buffalo who was edging him off the step in an attempt to gulp down the flowers floating on the surface.

Special Treatment

Dhobi tried every medication sold in the local dispensary to get rid of itchy scalp: Ayurvedic preparations, homeopathic concoctions, castor oil, linseed oil, mustard. He tried yogic exercises such as standing on his head for ten minutes three times a day. When his hair started to fall out he had a good excuse to visit the local herb doctor. But he couldn't stop that exasperating itch.

"Dandruff! It must be dandruff," the doctor concluded, handing Dhobi yet another gooey cream rinse.

Dhobi dutifully took it down to the river and

bathed in the usual way, following up with the cream rinse. It was so slimy, however, he had trouble rinsing it *out* of his hair. River silt clung to the strands. He had to buy a large-toothed comb to ply his way through the mess.

It was then that he made a startling discovery. Ambling down between the teeth of the comb was a large chunk of dandruff. Dhobi looked closer.

"Ah-ha!" he exclaimed. "Head lice! I should have known."

A special lice treatment was available in the bazaar. For twenty-five paisa Dhobi could rent a monkey on a leash. The monkey meticulously picked through Dhobi's scalp singling out the vermin and expertly popped them into his mouth. With smacking lips, the monkey scrunched the lice between his teeth like pomegranate seeds, juice squirting all over.

A Sound and Light Show

When a birth-control clinic opened nearby it was a huge success. Villagers came from miles around just to step on the automatic door mats and see the doors swing open. Inside a sound and light show illuminated the various methods of contraception in six dialects using life-sized models of people. A full selection of new products bearing the names of prominent movie stars was available: Agni Diaphragms, Prakash Condoms. The best-seller was a Hanuman Prophylactic which came with a full-color portrait of the Monkey God in one of his heroic poses. A display table illustrated the prizes and incentive awards that everyone was eligible for.

Dhobi asked himself over and over again the big question, "Is a vasectomy worth a transistor radio set?"

The Art of Washing Clothes

Dhobi learned meditation from his uncle who became a monk in the Vipassana tradition. Dhobi found he could incorporate the watching of his breath and bodily movements while washing his clothes on the banks of the river. He was in this conscious state of squeezing, sudsing, wringing, and rinsing his clothes when he was spotted by a group of hippies searching for a guru. They were immediately hypnotized by the transcendental manner of his washing. Even with their limited experience they could tell that this was no ordinary washerman.

Soon "The Art of Washing Clothes as a Means to Enlightenment" became a lively topic of discussion in the tea stalls along the river. It wasn't long before Dhobi could be seen sitting in a lotus posture on a bluff overlooking the river while below the aspirants perfected the art of washing clothes.

Dhobi's fame, thus far confined to this international group of travelers, diminished when the majority were expelled from the country after a periodic round-up of foreigners revealed that many held expired visas. Dhobi was perplexed by the loss of his helpers. As the last busload of travelers was setting off for the border, Dhobi waved from the station.

"Isn't the search for enlightenment more important than passbooks stamped in red?" he asked the Commissioner of Police.

There was no reply.

Dhobi at the Laundromat

When a laundromat opened in a nearby village Dhobi was one of the first to experience this modern convenience. He selected a large batch of his best clothing for the occasion – they weren't even dirty.

"Take mine, too!" his wife panted, running

after him with her wedding sari.

When Dhobi approached the building, a crowd of pilgrims was blocking the door. Mantras directed to Shiva rang out. A line formed and Dhobi fell into place behind the thirty-ninth person toting bundles of dirty laundry. By late afternoon his turn finally came. Dhobi asked a special favor... Could he have a small portion of the water as a keepsake?

The proprietors complied, accepting a bottle from his outstretched hand, and the magic cycle began: Soak/Wash/Rinse/Spin. Some water was procured from Rinse for Dhobi who muttered his thanks as though he were accepting communion from the village priest. The wet clothes were then loaded onto the back of Dhobi's mule for the trip back to the *ghat* where Dhobi would stretch each article over the banks to dry.

Sooner or Later

Sooner or later it was bound to happen. Dhobi was losing his customers to the new laundromat in the village. Could a man compete with a porcelain-white, automatic washing box? Apparently not. Even his sons refused to learn the trade of their father. They objected to getting their hands wet and abhorred smearing the clothes with soap on the sandstone steps of the river. Business was very slow.

Dhobi took the advice of his priest and began a series of prayer readings and offerings to Lakshmi. The priest, in describing an offering of "white rice clusters," was overheard by a passing anthropologist whose rudimentary knowledge of the dialect led him to decipher "mid-life crisis" and pull from his bag a list of ninety-six prepared questions.

In the months that followed, the anthropologist set up a complete study. Soon villagers flocked to Dhobi's hut on the banks of the river – mainly to view the anthropologist. Thus a calamity was averted and the washing business doubled.

A Cross-Cultural Survey

Shortly after an anthropologist began a survey of Dhobi's washing trade, the local chapter of the Indian Secret Service learned of this prolonged collaboration involving a foreigner. An officer was dispatched to Dhobi's *ghat* to investigate.

When he arrived, Dhobi was washing clothes and singing to himself, his song accentuated by the beat of the laundry paddle. The anthropologist, through the help of an informant, was trying to determine how many articles of clothing per stanza Dhobi washed, and in which order did he wash certain pieces. For instance, did a sari have preference over a dhoti? Was there a color factor involved?

The officer, so as not to arouse any suspicions, introduced himself as Dhobi's brother, slipping Dhobi a ten-rupee note to keep quiet. When the informant translated the news the anthropologist's eyes lit up. He was, in fact, anxious to expand his kinship survey.

In the days that followed, the anthropologist questioned the secret service officer disguised as Dhobi's brother. The officer, in turn, took copious notes on the other's questions. Dhobi was content collecting *baksheesh*, or small tips, from both parties.

No Laughing Matter

Dhobi's wife collects cowdung in a large basket perched on her head. At home, she kneads the dung with straw and slaps it into patties against the wall of their hut to dry. Dhobi pulls them off as needed to light the morning fire.

One morning after a rain Dhobi tossed into the fire two cowdung patties that had a fresh crop of mushrooms sprouting off to one side.

"Oh well," he reasoned. "Wood is scarce. I'm sure these will burn" — and didn't give it another thought.

Shortly afterwards a cloud of smoke rose up and filled the room. Dhobi was overcome with coughing. Then laughter. Then tears. He began to visualize Shiva, the Destroyer of the Universe, dancing wildly in front of him. When Dhobi joined in with a frenzy of movement and a babble of words, his wife, greatly upset, fled in search of the village exorcist.

Upon their return, Dhobi was cowering in a corner growling like a dog. Red betel juice dripping from his mouth reminded the priest of a vengeful blood-drooling Kali. A hideous laugh rang out.

Without further delay, the priest began an exorcism. Lighting incense, he recited the appropriate verses, dunking Dhobi's head in a bucket of water three times while blowing on a conch shell. Red chilies were put on the fire. Dhobi's wife prayed fervently by his side. Dhobi came around after inhaling the fumes of boiled cow urine although his throat was raw and his vision still blurred. He wasted no time in discrediting a rival washerman who no doubt was responsible for such witchery.

The Shivaratri Festival in Kathmandu is the destination of pilgrims throughout North India. What better way to spend "Lord Shiva's Night" than by blasting chillum after chillum in honor of the blue-throated god. *Bom Shankar!*

Dhobi spent two days camped on the railway station platform in preparation for the trip. His preparation consisted of watching the comings and goings of travelers at the station. He wanted to be extra sure of the procedure before striking out on his own. Third Class Unreserved was in theory "first come first served." In actual practice, however, it was who pushed hardest who managed to get inside the car. All others had to hang on the outside.

When the train pulled in, Dhobi was prepared. As planned he was among the first to crowd into the car — but at what expense! No sooner had he sat down when he realized something was missing — his wallet. Someone had picked his pocket in the stampede to get in.

What a dilemma! If he left to get a new ticket he'd lose his place. If he stayed without one he'd risk eviction from the car. Then Dhobi remembered, his money too was stolen. That settled it, there was no way to procure a ticket before the conductor came through. Dhobi sat still and rehearsed his appeal as the miles clacked by.

Mulberry Trees

Dhobi first came across mulberries in Almora on his way to Kathmandu. Holding their skirts like satchels, village women offered him some. Silkworms thrive on the leaves of the mulberry tree. Dhobi learned that silkworm production was an enterprise being taught to the local Tibetan refugees. It seemed a practical plan as silk was a good export item and spinning and weaving a valuable skill.

Any time you have a refugee situation, however, the word "rehabilitation" crops up. In this case, rehabilitation meant learning to kill because in order to procure the silk thread from the cocoons, the cocoons had to be first dropped into a boiling substance. The worm was killed in the process. For the Buddhist refugess, to kill the smallest insect, including a silkworm inside a cocoon, was a sin. To drop countless cocoons to their scalding death in order to unravel enough silk for a piece of cloth was equivalent to countless sins. And no one was going to risk rebirth in one of the eighteen hells over a piece of see-through cloth, no matter how sheer it was. Thus Dhobi was dissuaded from buying a gift for his wife.

Monsoon Plumbing

Even though there was a toilet in his village, Dhobi actually preferred the outdoors. He listened to the wind in the bamboo, the play of shadows in the cornfield — to name a few of the added attractions.

It was while squatting in a field that Dhobi first saw a fly give birth to larva. In the mountains he discovered round worms feasting in a mound of fresh baby crap. Dogs lapped up diarrhea as if it were warm milk. In cold climates he'd look for steam rising from it. In Orissa he had a pet dung beetle.

Dhobi's landlord in Almora showed him a dried-up waterfall a short walk from the house. This proved a boon in the monsoon season — every time it rained, it washed everything downhill.

Prison Reformed

A former security ward of a Nepalese Mental Hospital was transformed into a Buddhist monastery. Dhobi visited the compound on the outskirts of Kathmandu.

"The body is like a prison," said one of the devotees. "The cells with barred windows are fine for meditation. Our monks can gain freedom without stepping outside. It is of their own free will that they stay inside, locking out the distractions of a corrupt world."

Too bad it wasn't the other way around, Dhobi thought, with the prison made out of a former Buddhist monastery. The cells for the criminally insane could be fashioned out of rooms that once housed meditating monks. Faint traces of incense would permeate the halls. Visions of serene Buddhists would haunt the riotous frenzy of condemned minds. Graffiti would be mantras chiseled out of the walls.

A Dog's Life in Kathmandu

Every year one day is set aside to worship dogs in Kathmandu. Flower wreaths are woven for their heads and verses are recited praising ancestral canine heros. But it is a short-lived respite from the usual blows and curses. Few dogs are pets in Nepal, most are strays. When the King ordered the streets cleared of beggars and strays for the upcoming marriage of the Crown Prince, Dhobi saw poisoned meat set in strategic alleyways. For days dog carcasses cluttered the streets.

At the Tibetan monastery the dogs were poisoned ritually without their knowing it. Cakes of barley, sugar, and butter were ritually imbued with all the diseases of the valley: smallpox, malaria, cholera, and TB. So when the dogs ate the offering cakes, they ate the germs, too.

"That is why," the lamas said, "they are plagued with mange and running pus sores. Rabies is only a matter of time."

Dhobi's Inheritance

When Dhobi's aunt left him a modest inherittance, the first thing Dhobi could think of to do with the money, besides paying off the *chai wallah* and the *pan* and the *bidi* seller, was to go out and celebrate. So unexpected was this gift that it took him three days to decide to invest in a cycle rickshaw, thus enhancing his business prospects as well as providing transport for his family.

Dhobi quickly found new laundry customers but he had to work twice as hard to keep up. Not having the funds to hire someone else to pull him, he had to pedal himself after a full day of washing. By evening he was exhausted.

During Durga Puja festivities he sacrificed a chicken in honor of Durga, pouring a small amount of fresh blood and a few feathers on the front fender of the rickshaw, but it didn't prevent a collision. To avoid ramming a Brahmin cow one day, Dhobi swerved into a cabbage vendor. As cabbages rolled down the street the vendor had to beat off hungry cows with a handy stick. He would have beaten Dhobi, too, if Dhobi hadn't bought the toppled produce.

Thus Dhobi was spared any further embarrassment in the market, but he struggled to keep the cabbages from rolling off the seat as he pedaled home. For two weeks Dhobi ate cabbage curry, cabbage fritters, boiled, stewed, sautéed, and pickled cabbage with stuffed *samosas*. To anyone who asked, it was just another meatless week.

A Severe Drought

Dhobi's mule, by circumstance a scavenger, was having a harder and harder time locating grass and odd leaves. Hours of grazing turned up only a mouthful of twigs. The countryside was suffering from the worst drought in years. A once fertile river basin was quickly turned into a dust bowl.

Grass being so scarce, the mule soon developed a taste for newsprint. Dhobi did his best to save the outer cabbage leaves, carrot tops, and discarded potato skins, but, lacking these, the colorful comic strip page in the Sunday newspaper was second best.

Water was rationed and faucets turned on only once a day. Village wells ran dry. The river sank so low that entire temple compounds sunken many years ago were uncovered. When two statues of Durga turned up, a ceremony was initiated by the local pundi, who feared the wrath of the goddess was responsible for the lack of rain.

Dhobi had an insight into the cruel forces of karma when three village cows died of starvation. He watched from a nearby hill as vultures ripped into the carcasses and fought greedily over the rotting flesh. They gorged themselves until, too full to fly, they moped around in a stupor. Some performed victory dances; others vomited undigested carrion. It was then that Dhobi could walk among them undisturbed. Shaking his head in disgust, he muttered to himself.

"While gaunt cows die of starvation, vultures thrive and multiply."

Cover-Up

When a wave-cyclone disaster struck the countryside, Dhobi heard that the official dead count was over 8,000. Rampant gossip, however, carried the figure upwards to 50,000. The government offered to help with the clean-up but their offer of ten rupees per body was rejected by soldiers, policemen, and private contractors alike when it was learned that the majority of victims was untouchables.

An uproar ensued. While officials in governing circles adamantly proclaimed that caste discrimination was illegal and obsolete, corpses lay decomposing in the fields. Finally one politician suggested a solution.

"Why not recruit the convicts from the nearby Central Prison to bury the bodies in exchange for a reduced sentence?"

The plan was implemented and fifty convicts were selected to participate. Dhobi's nephew wrote from the prison.

"At first we were happy for a chance to reduce our sentences," he said. "But by the time we finish burying the alloted one hundred and fifty odd bodies each, using only simple hand tools, there won't be any time left in my sentence to commute."

The Memsahib's Legacy

On the basis of a rumor that beef was available, a well-heeled memsahib ventured into the Muslim quarter in hopes of procuring the illicit meat. In the midst of her haggling over the price, once she had found a seller, the zipper of her trousers suddenly gave way — if ever one's life depended on a zipper, it was now. The act of clutching her waist to keep the trousers up offended Muslim proprieties. A crowd formed around her. Offended men jeered while others aired their versions of the incident. A small riot broke out and a stone was hurled in her direction.

It was just at this point that Dhobi, returning from delivering a bundle of freshly laundered clothes, pedaled by on his new cycle rickshaw. The memsahib, seeing an empty vehicle of escape, quickly hopped in just as a rock whizzed past Dhobi's head. He didn't need any persuasion to speed off, but he meant to tell the lady that he didn't carry passengers since he was only a washer man by trade.

When they had traveled a good distance from the gathering mob, the memsahib motioned Dhobi to stop. She handed him a five-rupee note and tossed in a jar of hand cream to show her appreciation.

By the gleam of the silver label and the manner of the fair-skinned lady, Dhobi figured it was a special skin lightener and duly presented it to his wife. She kept it as a trophy for all to see on her shrine. And after receiving two offers to buy the

American-made product, she realized its worth. And black market or no black market, she was going to keep it.

Dreams of a Chinese Laundry

Dhobi was not one to complain. He endured the daily trudge to the river, the slap and bang of the paddle beating the grime out of the laundry, the inevitable sand that got into the clothes he was trying to clean. Generation after generation of washermen had perfected the art of clothes washing but secretly Dhobi could think of nothing better than to have his own shop — automatic machines that would do all the work for him.

There was talk of the countries in the west with many Chinese laundries. If only he could emigrate, he might work in a Chinese laundry. He'd buy shoes and full pants.

The Chinese laundry dream rose like a lotus from the depths of Dal Lake. He began to plan for it. He'd build his own Chinese laundry with a pagoda roof and a dragon door. Inside the walls could be painted red with chrysanthemum and peony borders. A display case could house plastic flowers in blue willow vases. Every week he would send money home. He'd burn incense and eat with chopsticks. Maybe he could serve fortune

cookies on Chinese New Year and save for a bro-
cade jacket.

How a Toilet Became a Museum

Once a well-meaning group devoted to international health brought a portable toilet into Dhobi's
village. The molded yellow plastic module was
erected in the central square near the bathing tank
and water supply. It seemed an accessible spot.

However, the health-conscious director of the
group knew nothing of the prevailing defecatory
practices. Of the whole village, only the lowly
sweepers were authorized, or assigned, the grim
chore of carrying out the excrement and cleaning
the toilets. Because of their polluting work, the
sweepers were never allowed to walk in front of
the main shrine which was on the path to the village square where the newly installed toilet was.
To set foot in the central square itself was unheard
of.

So with no one to service the toilets, no one
dared use them — to say nothing of the curious
seat on which one is supposed to rest their thighs.
But villagers from the surrounding area make a
point of stopping off to view this foreign contrap-
tion and if they have a few rupees to spare, they'll
line up for a still portrait in front of the "museum"

(as it is now called) by the man with an antique tripod camera who has taken to standing nearby.